JANEEN SARLIN

Roasts

Photography by SIMON WHEELER

THE MASTER CHEFS

TED SMART

JANEEN A SARLIN is the owner and president of Cooking with Class, a New York City catering company and cooking school established in 1975. She is a syndicated food columnist, gives lectures and teaches cooking classes across the United States and produces a weekly radio programme, *The Seasonal Chef.*

Janeen is a member of the International Association of Culinary Professionals, The American Institute of Wine and Food, The James Beard Foundation, Les Dames d'Escoffier, The New York Woman's Culinary Alliance and The International Association of Women Chefs.

Raised on a dairy farm in Minnesota, she learned the basic traditions and secrets of roasting from her grandmother and mother. Janeen is the author of *Lunches To Go* (1984) and *Food From An American Farm* (1991).

CONTENTS

There are no secrets

in cooking, but let

me tell you a few!

INTRODUCTION

Roasting is an old technique that fits right into today's style of cooking. The preparation time is relatively short and while the food is roasting in the oven, one can accomplish other tasks. In addition, the presentation of a splendid roast at the dinner table is guaranteed to impress.

Whether it's meat, poultry, fish or vegetables, these recipes show how roasting renders the outside crisp and brown and the inside moist and succulent, and intensifies the original flavours of the food.

Different spices and herbs have been chosen to complement the flavours of the roasts: fragrant coriander seeds form a crust on succulent salmon; a coat of peppercorns gives a spicy taste to crisp duck skin; fresh green mint and watercress are perfect for a springtime leg of lamb; tarragon subtly emphasizes the flavour of a tender fillet of beef. In Pomander Chicken the warm, spicy aromas of orange, cloves and cinnamon permeate the meat from the inside.

Try a few of my favourite recipes and find out how simple it is to produce mouthwatering roasts with minimum effort.

Daveen A. Darten

ROSEMARY ROASTED VEGETABLES

6–7 TABLESPOONS EXTRA VIRGIN
   OLIVE OIL
3 LARGE BAKING POTATOES,
   SCRUBBED
3 TABLESPOONS FRESH ROSEMARY,
   BRUISED
COARSE SALT
FRESHLY GROUND BLACK PEPPER
3 LARGE ONIONS
450 G/1 LB BABY CARROTS, PEELED
450 G/1 LB ASPARAGUS, PEELED
   AND TOUGH ENDS REMOVED

*Almost any combination of vegetables can
be used: try parsnips, aubergines, peppers.
Roasting times may vary, depending on
the variety, size and age of the vegetables,
so check them every so often. Roast one
vegetable at a time and be sure to stir or
turn them over occasionally so that they
brown on all sides.*

SERVES 6

Preheat the oven to 200°C/
400°F/Gas Mark 6. Lightly grease
four baking sheets with olive oil.

Cut the potatoes into quarters
lengthways. Place them on one of
the baking sheets, cut side down.

Drizzle with olive oil and sprinkle
on a little rosemary, salt and
pepper. Roast for 50 minutes–
1 hour or until tender when tested
with the point of a fork.

Keeping the skin on the
onions, trim off the roots but leave
the root end intact. Cut into
quarters and place cut side down
on a baking sheet. Drizzle with
olive oil, rosemary, salt and pepper.
Roast for about 45 minutes or
until the onions are browned,
caramelized and soft. Peel off the
skin before serving.

Arrange the carrots in a single
layer on a baking sheet. Drizzle
with olive oil, rosemary, salt and
pepper. Roast for about 45 minutes
or until tender when tested with
the point of a fork.

Arrange the asparagus in a
single layer on a baking sheet.
Drizzle with olive oil, rosemary,
salt and pepper. Roast for 15–20
minutes or until tender when
tested with the point of a fork.

To serve as a side dish, arrange
the roasted vegetables on a platter
and reheat if necessary. To serve as
a first course, toss with hot pasta.

CORIANDER-CRUSTED SALMON
and leeks

2–3 TABLESPOONS EXTRA VIRGIN
  OLIVE OIL

1 STICK OF CELERY, CHOPPED

25 G/1 OZ BUTTER

3 LEEKS (MOSTLY WHITE PART), CUT
  INTO FINE STRIPS

85 ML/3 FL OZ WHITE WINE

COARSE SALT

FRESHLY GROUND BLACK PEPPER

1.6 KG/3½ LB WHOLE SALMON,
  SCALED AND GUTTED (OR A TAIL
  OR CENTRE-CUT SECTION)

2 TABLESPOONS CRUSHED
  CORIANDER SEEDS

FRESH PARSLEY, TO GARNISH

SERVES 6

Preheat the oven to 200°C/400°F/ Gas Mark 6. Lightly grease a large baking sheet with olive oil. Spread the celery over the baking sheet.

Melt the butter in a saucepan and add the leeks and wine. Cover and cook over very low heat until the leeks are limp, about 5 minutes. Season to taste and leave to cool.

Generously season the fish inside and out. Place half of the leeks inside the fish and scatter the remainder over the celery. Place the fish on the bed of vegetables.

Drizzle olive oil over the fish, then press coriander seeds into the skin on the top side of the fish to form a crust.

Roast the fish for 20–30 minutes (about 10 minutes per 2.5 cm/1 inch thickness.) The fish is done when it is aromatic, the skin on the tail bubbles, and there is no raw red colour near the bone when pierced with a skewer.

Transfer the fish to a warm platter and serve with the roasted leeks. Garnish with parsley.

POMANDER CHICKEN

3 TANGERINES OR MINNEOLAS
12 WHOLE CLOVES
2 STICKS OF CELERY, CHOPPED
1 LARGE ROASTING CHICKEN
  (ABOUT 3.4–3.6 KG/7½–8 LB),
  WASHED AND PATTED DRY
1 LIME, CUT IN HALF
COARSE SALT
FRESHLY GROUND BLACK PEPPER
15 CM/6 INCH CINNAMON STICK,
  BROKEN IN HALF
85 G/3 OZ BUTTER, SOFTENED
ABOUT 125 ML/4 FL OZ CHICKEN
  STOCK
85 ML/3 FL OZ FRESH ORANGE
  JUICE

SERVES 6–8
Preheat the oven to 220°C/425°F/
Gas Mark 7. Slice off the tops and
bottoms of two of the tangerines
and stud each with six cloves. Pare
off the zest of the remaining
tangerine and cut into fine strips.

Spread the celery in a roasting
tin; set a rack over the celery. Rub
the skin and inside the chicken
with the lime; season with salt and
pepper. Place the tangerines and
the cinnamon inside the chicken.

Mix half the butter with the
strips of zest. Gently lift the skin
from the breast and thighs and
push the tangerine butter under
the skin. Rub the remaining butter
over the chicken. Truss and place
on the rack, breast down.

Roast for 35–45 minutes or
until the skin is brown. Turn breast
side up and continue roasting for
about 35 minutes or until the
breast skin is brown. Once the skin
is crisp, baste with the juices.

Reduce the oven temperature
to 180°C/350°F/Gas Mark 4 and
roast the chicken for a further
1–1½ hours, basting occasionally,
until the juices run clear when the
thigh is pierced with a skewer.
Leave to rest in a warm place for
20–25 minutes before carving.

Pour the roasting tin juices into
a jug or fat strainer and leave for 5
minutes. Pour off the fat, then pour
the juices into a saucepan and add
enough stock to make up 125 ml/
4 fl oz. Add the orange juice and
simmer for a few minutes. Add the
juices from the resting roast.
Reheat the sauce and serve with
the chicken.

GARLIC-STUDDED ROAST BEEF

3.2–3.4 KG/7–7¼ LB FORERIB OF
BEEF, ON THE BONE, CHINED★

2 WHOLE GARLIC CLOVES, CUT
INTO SLIVERS

½ TEASPOON DRIED CHILLI FLAKES

1 TEASPOON FRESHLY GROUND
BLACK PEPPER

½ TEASPOON COARSE SALT

2 CARROTS, CHOPPED

2 ONIONS, CHOPPED

ABOUT 125 ML/4 FL OZ BEEF
STOCK

★ *Buy the beef up to 5 days in advance.
Trim off any excess fat and leave in the
refrigerator, uncovered, to dry-age for at
least 24 hours (or up to 5 days). Before
roasting, shave off the dried ends with a
sharp knife. Tie between the ribs with
kitchen string.*

SERVES 6–8

Using the point of a small knife,
cut slits in the meat and stud with
slivers of garlic. Crush the chilli
flakes together with the black
pepper. Rub the salt and the
pepper mixture into the meat.
Leave to stand at room
temperature for 30 minutes.

Preheat the oven to 240°C/
475°F/Gas Mark 9. Strew the
carrots and onions in a roasting tin
and set a rack over the vegetables.
Place the beef on the rack and
roast for 30 minutes.

Reduce the oven temperature
to 180°C/350°F/Gas Mark 4 and
continue roasting the beef for a
further 1–1½ hours, until the meat
is done to your liking. Leave to rest
for 20–25 minutes before carving.

Pour the roasting tin juices into
a jug or fat strainer and leave for 5
minutes. Pour off the fat, then pour
the juices into a saucepan and add
enough stock to make up 125 ml/
4 fl oz. Simmer for a few minutes,
skimming off any fat. Add the
juices from the resting roast.
Reheat the sauce and serve with
the beef.

PEPPER DUCK

with brandy sauce

2 DUCKS, ABOUT 1.6–1.8 KG/
    3½–4 LB EACH, EXCESS FAT
    REMOVED, WASHED, PATTED DRY
1 LEMON, CUT IN HALF
COARSE SALT
2–2½ TABLESPOONS MIXED BLACK
    AND WHITE PEPPERCORNS,
    CRUSHED
ZEST OF 1 LARGE ORANGE AND
    ½ LARGE GRAPEFRUIT
2 STICKS OF CELERY, CHOPPED
125 ML/4 FL OZ BRANDY

SERVES 8

Rub the skin and inside the ducks with the lemon and season with salt and a generous pinch of the crushed peppercorns. Cut the orange and grapefruit zest into fine strips and blanch in boiling water for 2 minutes, then pat dry. Place half of the celery, orange and grapefruit zest in the cavity of each duck and truss the ducks. Using a two-pronged fork, prick the ducks all over, making more holes in fatty areas. Rub the remaining peppercorns all over the ducks, then leave to stand at room temperature for 30 minutes.

Preheat the oven to 230°C/450°F/Gas Mark 8. Set a rack in a roasting tin.

Roast the ducks on the rack, breast side down, for 15–20 minutes or until the skin is brown. Turn breast side up and continue roasting for 15–20 minutes or until the breast skin is brown and crisp. Pour out the fat from the tin.

Reduce the oven temperature to 200°C/400°F/Gas Mark 6 and roast the ducks for a further 1–1½ hours, piercing the skin several times to release the excess fat. Occasionally you will need to pour out more fat from the bottom of the tin. The ducks are done when the drumsticks move up and down easily and the inside juices are no longer red. Leave to rest for 15–20 minutes before carving.

Pour out all but 1 tablespoon of the fat and peppercorns from the tin. Place the tin over medium heat and add the brandy. Stir well to deglaze and simmer until syrupy.

Using poultry shears, cut on either side of the backbone and discard. Cut each duck half into two and serve with the sauce.

CALIFORNIA LOIN OF PORK
with mango, date and apple salsa

2.4–3 KG/5½–6 LB BONELESS LOIN
  OF PORK, WELL TRIMMED AND
  TIED EVERY 5 CM/2 INCHES
3 PIECES OF CRYSTALLIZED GINGER,
  CUT INTO SLIVERS
ZEST OF 1 LIME, CUT INTO FINE
  STRIPS
1 SMALL ONION, SLICED
1 BOTTLE FULL-BODIED RED WINE
1 TABLESPOON FRESH ROSEMARY
  OR 1½ TEASPOONS DRIED
1½ TEASPOONS FRESHLY GROUND
  BLACK PEPPER
½ TEASPOON COARSE SALT

MANGO, DATE AND APPLE SALSA

2 LARGE MANGOES, DICED
12 LARGE FRESH DATES, PITTED
  AND CHOPPED
2 LARGE, FIRM, TART APPLES
  (GRANNY SMITH), PEELED,
  CORED AND CHOPPED
3 TABLESPOONS SNIPPED CHIVES
2 TABLESPOONS CHOPPED
  CRYSTALLIZED GINGER
JUICE OF 3 LARGE LIMES
ABOUT 4 TABLESPOONS EXTRA
  VIRGIN OLIVE OIL

SERVES 10–12

Using the point of a small knife, cut slits in the meat and stud with slivers of ginger. Place in a shallow, non-reactive dish, add the lime zest and onion and pour over the wine. Cover and marinate for 2 hours at room temperature or overnight in the refrigerator. Bring back to room temperature before roasting.

Preheat the oven to 220°C/ 425°F/Gas Mark 8. Set a rack in a roasting tin.

Remove the meat from the marinade and pat dry. Chop the rosemary together with the pepper and salt. Rub the seasonings all over the pork, then place on the rack, fat side up.

Roast for 45 minutes or until the meat begins to brown. Reduce the oven temperature to 180°C/ 350°F/Gas Mark 4 and continue roasting for a further 1½ hours.

Meanwhile, make the salsa: mix all the ingredients together, add pepper to taste, and add enough olive oil to bind the mixture.

Leave the pork to rest for 15–20 minutes before carving, then serve with the salsa.

LEG OF LAMB
with mint and watercress

2 BUNCHES OF WATERCRESS
    LEAVES, COARSELY CHOPPED
2 SMALL BUNCHES OF FRESH
    SPEARMINT LEAVES, COARSELY
    CHOPPED
1 LARGE BUNCH OF FLAT LEAF
    PARSLEY LEAVES, COARSELY
    CHOPPED
3 GARLIC CLOVES, CHOPPED
125–150 ML/4–5 FL OZ OLIVE OIL
COARSE SALT
FRESHLY GROUND BLACK PEPPER
2 ONIONS, SLICED
3–3.2 KG/6–7 LB LEG OF LAMB,
    TRIMMED OF ALL EXCESS FAT
250 ML/8 FL OZ CHICKEN STOCK
SPRIGS OF WATERCRESS, TO
    GARNISH

SERVES 6–8

Place the watercress, mint, parsley and garlic in a food processor and pulse briefly. With the machine running, pour the olive oil through the feeder tube to make a stiff, spreadable paste. Season with salt and pepper to taste.

Preheat the oven to 230°/450°F/Gas Mark 8. Strew the onions in a roasting tin and set a rack over them.

Season the lamb, then, using a spatula, spread the herb mixture all over the meat. Place the lamb on the rack and roast for 30 minutes.

Reduce the oven temperature to 180°C/350°F/Gas Mark 4 and continue roasting for a further 30 minutes–1 hour. Leave to rest for 15–20 minutes before carving.

Pour the stock into the hot roasting tin and stir well to deglaze. Pour into a jug or fat strainer and leave for 5 minutes. Pour off the fat, then pour the juices into a saucepan and simmer for a few minutes, skimming off any fat. Add the juices from the resting roast. Reheat the sauce and serve with the lamb. Garnish with watercress.

ROAST VEAL DIJON

1.6–1.8 KG/3½–4 LB BONELESS TOP
 RUMP OF VEAL, TRIMMED AND
 TIED
1 TEASPOON MUSTARD SEEDS
1 TEASPOON WHOLE BLACK
 PEPPERCORNS
500 ML/16 FL OZ MILK
2 TEASPOONS DRIED TARRAGON
FRESHLY GROUND BLACK PEPPER
225 G/8 OZ DIJON MUSTARD
5 TABLESPOONS BUTTER, MELTED
85 ML/3 FL OZ DRY SHERRY
85 ML/3 FL OZ CHICKEN STOCK
2 SHALLOTS, CHOPPED
1 TART GREEN APPLE, PEELED,
 CORED AND SLICED
FLAT LEAF PARSLEY, TO GARNISH

SERVES 6

Soak the veal, mustard seeds and
peppercorns in the milk overnight
in the refrigerator.

Discard the marinade, rinse the
veal and pat dry with paper towels.
Rub the meat with the tarragon
and freshly ground black pepper.

Preheat the oven to 160°C/
325°/Gas Mark 3. Place the meat
in a roasting tin. Beat the Dijon
mustard with 4 tablespoons of the
melted butter and pour over the
meat, to cover on all sides. Roast
for 2½ hours.

Reduce the oven temperature
to 150°C/300°F/Gas Mark 2 and
continue to roast the veal for about
1 hour, basting every 15 minutes
with sherry and chicken stock.
Leave to rest for 15–20 minutes
before slicing.

While the veal is roasting, heat
the remaining 1 tablespoon butter
in a small saucepan and sauté the
chopped shallots until soft. Add the
apple slices and sauté until just
tender but still holding their shape.
Set aside.

Add the juices from the
roasting tin to the shallot and apple
mixture and simmer for a few
minutes to reduce and enrich the
flavour of the sauce.

Garnish the carved veal with
parsley. Serve the sauce separately.

TENDERLOIN OF BEEF

1 WHOLE FILLET OF BEEF, WELL
  TRIMMED (ABOUT 1.8 KG/4 LB
  AFTER TRIMMING)
1 TABLESPOON COARSELY GROUND
  BLACK PEPPER
1½ TEASPOONS DRIED TARRAGON
1 TEASPOON HERBES DE PROVENCE
3 TABLESPOONS COGNAC
ABOUT 1 TABLESPOON EXTRA
  VIRGIN OLIVE OIL
175 ML/6 FL OZ BEEF STOCK

SERVES 6–8

Rub the meat with pepper,
tarragon and herbes de Provence.
Fold the thin tail-end under and
tie with kitchen string every 5 cm/
2 inches. Place the beef in a
roasting tin. Drizzle 2 tablespoons
of the Cognac over the meat.
Leave to stand at room
temperature for 30 minutes.

Preheat the oven to 240°C/
475°F/Gas Mark 9. Rub olive oil
all over the meat and roast for
exactly 30 minutes for rare, 35
minutes for medium rare.

Remove the roast from the
oven and wrap in nonstick baking
paper, folding the edges of the
paper together to make a sealed
parcel. Then roll up the parcel in
several thicknesses of newspaper
and leave to rest for 20–25 minutes
before slicing.

Place the roasting tin over
medium-high heat, pour in the
beef stock and stir well to deglaze
while bringing to the boil. Pour
into a jug or fat strainer and leave
to stand for 5 minutes. Pour off the
fat, then pour the juices into a
saucepan. Add the remaining
Cognac and simmer for a few
minutes, skimming off any fat, to
reduce and enrich the flavour of
the sauce. Add the juices from the
resting beef. Reheat the sauce and
serve with the sliced beef. Garnish
with watercress.

ROAST TURKEY BURGUNDY

2 CARROTS, CHOPPED

2 LARGE ONIONS, CHOPPED

4 STICKS OF CELERY, CHOPPED

6–6.4 KG/12–14 LB FRESH TURKEY,
WASHED AND WIPED DRY
(GIBLETS MADE INTO STOCK)

1 LEMON, CUT IN HALF

COARSE SALT

FRESHLY GROUND BLACK PEPPER

3–4 LARGE FRESH SAGE LEAVES,
CHOPPED

4 TABLESPOONS SOFTENED BUTTER

SAUSAGE STUFFING (PAGE 28),
OPTIONAL

1 BOTTLE BURGUNDY WINE

SERVES 12

Preheat the oven to 220°C/425°F/
Gas Mark 7. Strew the carrots,
onions and celery in a roasting tin
and set a rack over them.

Rub the skin and inside the
turkey with the lemon, then season
generously with salt and pepper.
Mix the sage with the butter.
Using your fingers, carefully
separate the skin from the breast
and thighs. Push half the butter
under the skin. Rub the remaining
butter all over the turkey.

Either place a handful of the
chopped vegetables inside the
turkey or stuff with Sausage
Stuffing. Truss the turkey and place
on the rack, breast side down.

Roast breast side down for
20–30 minutes or until the skin is
brown. Turn on to one side and
roast for 20 minutes, then turn on
to the other side for a further 20
minutes. Finally, turn the bird
breast side up and continue
roasting until the skin is brown.
Once the skin is crisp, begin
basting with some of the wine.

Reduce the oven temperature
to 180°C/350°F/Gas Mark 4 and
roast for a further 2½–3 hours,
basting occasionally with the wine,
until the juices run clear when the
meat is pierced with a fork and the
thighs move freely. Leave to rest for
20–25 minutes before carving.

Pour the roasting tin juices into
a jug or fat strainer and leave for 5
minutes. Pour off the fat, then pour
the juices into a saucepan. Simmer
for a few minutes, skimming off
any fat. Add the juices from the
resting roast. Reheat the sauce and
serve with the turkey.

THE BASICS

SAUSAGE STUFFING

3 TABLESPOONS BUTTER
2 LARGE ONIONS, CHOPPED
225 G/8 OZ WHITE RICE
1 LITRE/1¾ PINTS HOT CHICKEN
  STOCK
900 G/2 LB SPICY ITALIAN
  SAUSAGES
6 WHOLE GARLIC CLOVES
2–4 TABLESPOONS OLIVE OIL
1 LARGE GREEN PEPPER, DICED
1 LARGE RED PEPPER, DICED
225 G/8 OZ MUSHROOMS, SLICED
SPLASH OF MADEIRA OR PORT
25–40 G/1–1½ OZ FRESH FLAT
  LEAF PARSLEY, CHOPPED
1–2 TABLESPOONS CHOPPED FRESH
  SAGE
2 TEASPOONS FRESH MARJORAM
50 G/2 OZ PINE NUTS, TOASTED
SALT AND FRESHLY GROUND PEPPER
675 G/1½ LB MOZZARELLA
  CHEESE, CUBED

**ENOUGH FOR A 6–6.4 KG/
12–14 LB TURKEY PLUS AN
EXTRA SIDE DISH**

Preheat the oven to 190°C/375°F/
Gas Mark 5. In a heavy-based
casserole, melt the butter and sauté
one of the onions until soft and
translucent. Add the rice and
continue to sauté until the rice is
translucent. Stir in the hot chicken
stock and bring to the boil. Cover
the casserole and place in the oven
for about 20 minutes, or until the
rice is just tender. Remove from
the oven and leave to cool slightly.

Meanwhile, place the sausages
and garlic in a saucepan with just
enough cold water to cover. Bring
to the boil, then reduce the heat
and simmer for about 20 minutes
or until the sausages are cooked.
Drain, discarding the water and

garlic. Slice the sausages and sauté in a frying pan with a little olive oil, until brown. Drain the sausages on paper towels, then transfer to a large bowl.

In the same frying pan, sauté the remaining onion until soft and translucent. Add the peppers and sauté until tender. Add to the bowl with the sausages.

In the same frying pan, adding more oil if necessary, sauté the mushrooms over high heat until they squeak. Drizzle the madeira or port over the mushrooms and boil for a few minutes, then add to the sausage mixture.

Chop the herbs together and mix into the rice, together with the pine nuts. Combine the herbed rice with the vegetable and sausage mixture. Mix well, taste and adjust the seasoning if required. Leave to cool to room temperature or chill in the refrigerator.

Just before stuffing the turkey, add the cubed mozzarella. Spoon into the turkey cavities, being careful not to overfill.

Place the remaining stuffing in a casserole and bake at 180°C/ 350°F/Gas Mark 4 for 30–40 minutes (while the turkey is resting) or until hot through and brown on top.

TECHNIQUES AND TIPS

Roasting food over a bed of vegetables helps to keep the roast moist and well-flavoured; the roasted vegetables then provide the basis for the accompanying gravy or sauce.

There are various ways (described in the recipes) to test that a roast is done. To use a meat thermometer, insert it into the thickest part of the meat.
Fish – 65°C/150°F.
Beef – 49–50°C/120°F for rare, 52–55°C/125–130°F for medium rare.
Lamb – 51–52°C/125°F for rosy rare, 54–55°C/130°F for medium pink.
Veal – 65–70°C/150–155°F.
Pork – about 70°C/155–160°F.
Chicken and turkey – about 75°C/165–170°F; test turkey in several places.

Marinating food before roasting can enhance the flavour and tenderize the meat. Meat that has been marinated must be thoroughly patted dry before roasting, so that when it goes into the hot oven the outside can quickly seal in the flavours.

Tying roasts evenly helps them keep an attractive shape and makes them easier to carve or slice. However, the string may sometimes pull away the delicious crusty outer layer, so take care, running a small sharp knife along the string before removing it.

The secret of perfect roast duck – where the meat is tender but not fatty and the skin is crisp – is to pierce the skin really thoroughly. As the bird cooks, the excess fat is released – and the duck bastes itself!

THE MASTER CHEFS

SOUPS
ARABELLA BOXER

MEZE, TAPAS AND ANTIPASTI
AGLAIA KREMEZI

PASTA SAUCES
GORDON RAMSAY

RISOTTO
MICHELE SCICOLONE

SALADS
CLARE CONNERY

MEDITERRANEAN
ANTONY WORRALL THOMPSON

VEGETABLES
PAUL GAYLER

LUNCHES
ALASTAIR LITTLE

COOKING FOR TWO
RICHARD OLNEY

FISH
RICK STEIN

CHICKEN
BRUNO LOUBET

SUPPERS
VALENTINA HARRIS

THE MAIN COURSE
ROGER VERGÉ

ROASTS
JANEEN SARLIN

WILD FOOD
ROWLEY LEIGH

PACIFIC
JILL DUPLEIX

CURRIES
PAT CHAPMAN

HOT AND SPICY
PAUL AND JEANNE RANKIN

THAI
JACKI PASSMORE

CHINESE
YAN-KIT SO

VEGETARIAN
KAREN LEE

DESSERTS
MICHEL ROUX

CAKES
CAROLE WALTER

COOKIES
ELINOR KLIVANS

THE MASTER CHEFS

This edition produced for The Book People Ltd,

Hall Wood Avenue, Haydock, St Helens WAII 9UL

Text © copyright 1996 Janeen A Sarlin

Photographs © copyright 1996 Simon Wheeler

First published in 1996 by

WEIDENFELD & NICOLSON

THE ORION PUBLISHING GROUP

ORION HOUSE

5 UPPER ST MARTIN'S LANE

LONDON WC2H 9EA

British Library Cataloguing-in-Publication data
A catalogue record for this book is available
from the British Library.

ISBN 0 297 83639 0

DESIGNED BY THE SENATE

EDITOR MAGGIE RAMSAY

FOOD STYLIST JOY DAVIES

ASSISTANT KATY HOLDER